BEFORE YOU SAY "I DO" GOD'S COUNSEL FOR PUR-POSEFUL MARRIAGE

By

Ose-Akhumen Momoh

Published by TOGLM Int'l Media Room
Lagos, Nigeria
© 2025 Ose-akhumen Momoh
All rights reserved.

📄 Copyright Page

Before You Say "I Do"
God's Counsel for Purposeful Marriage

Unless otherwise noted, Scripture quotations are taken from:

- *The Holy Bible, New King James Version® (NKJV)*. Copyright © 1982 by Thomas Nelson. Used by permission. All rights reserved.
- *The Holy Bible, King James Version (KJV)*. Public domain.

Cover designed by TOGLM Int'l Media Room
Interior layout by TOGLM Int'l Media Room
Printed in Nigeria

ISBN: 978-978-691-371-1
First Edition

For permissions, inquiries, or ministry resources, contact:
Email: toglmintl@gmail.com

📌 Publisher's Note

This book is published under the spiritual and editorial guidance of the Holy Spirit through His Grace, Prophet Ose-Akhumen Momoh. All content herein reflects the prophetic convictions, biblical insights, and pastoral counsel of Prophet Ose-Akhumen Momoh.

We believe this work is a timely tool for restoring homes, preparing hearts, and aligning marriages with heaven's blueprint. It is our prayer that every reader will encounter truth, healing, and divine clarity through these pages.

For permissions, ministry inquiries, or bulk orders, please contact:

Prophet Ose-Akhumen Momoh Ministries

Email: toglmintl@gmail.com

Tel: +2347030839594, +23480111084169

All glory to Jesus Christ, the Builder of every lasting home.

📖 Dedication

To God Almighty — my Refuge, my Strength, my Song.
You are the breath in my lungs and the fire in my bones.
All I am and all I will ever be is for Your glory.

To my dear **Igwemidere** and our precious children —
You are my earthly treasures.
Your love is a safe harbor, your faith a constant wind in my sails.
Together, we journey in God's purpose.

To the **unmarried** — may you walk into marriage with wisdom, not just excitement.

To the **engaged** — may you build on a foundation that will last.

To the **married** — may your union become a living sermon of God's faithfulness.

This book is for you —

a seed,

a mirror,

and a light on your path.

📖 Table of Contents

iv

Foreword

By Apostle Meshach Nwazue
President, Shekinah Missions

Marriage is one of God's most beautiful creations — a divine covenant, not just a human contract. Yet in today's world, many enter into it with excitement but without revelation. The result? Homes that look strong on the outside but are quietly crumbling within.

In *Before You Say "I Do"*, Prophet Ose-akhumen Momoh speaks with the voice of a shepherd, the wisdom of a counselor, and the urgency of a watchman. This is not a book of theories or recycled advice. It is a call — a prophetic call — to return to God's original blueprint for marriage.

Every page carries a weight of personal testimony, biblical truth, and practical counsel. The author does not shy away from the hard conversations: the silent struggles in homes, the misplaced priorities in relationships, and the spiritual attacks that target the unity of husband and wife. He also speaks with compassion to the unmarried, the engaged, and even the married who are hurting — offering guidance that is as timely as it is timeless.

Reading this book feels like sitting at the feet of a trusted spiritual father in the Lord who loves you enough to prepare you for both the beauty and the battles of marriage. It will challenge you, inspire you, and equip you to make decisions that please God and protect your destiny.

Whether you are single, preparing for marriage, newly married, or navigating storms in your home, this book is for you.

Do not just read it — receive it. Let its truths sink deep into your heart and shape the foundation of your relationship.

My prayer is that as you read, the Holy Spirit will open your eyes to see marriage as God sees it, your ears to hear His voice more clearly, and your heart to obey His leading.

Marriage is not just about love — it is about purpose, destiny, and the glory of God. May this book guide you into all three.

📖 Acknowledgements

First and foremost, I return all glory, honor, and praise to the Almighty God—the Author of life, the Giver of purpose, and the One who has woven my past, my present, and His divine plans into the inspiration for this book. Without Him, there would be no message, no mission, and no *Church in My House*.

To my beloved biological father in the Lord, of blessed memory, **Late Prophet C. O. Momoh**—your prophetic calling and ministry inspired me from birth. Your prayer requests concerning me were seeds of destiny; your prophecies never failed. Your unwavering faith and commitment to the Kingdom remain a guiding light to my steps.

To my dear spouse, **Igwemidere**, and my lovely children—your support has been nothing short of 101%. You have stood beside me through every prayer, every sleepless night, and every chapter of this journey. This book carries your fingerprints of love, patience, and faith.

To my family—I thank God for your encouragement and covering. To my missionary partners at **SHEKINAH Mission**, especially Apostle Meshach (President), and to all who have received impartation and healing through God's servant—by His grace, through my ministry—in prayers and counseling—your testimonies are the fruit of divine grace. Your steadfastness and labors in the Lord are never in vain.

To the ministries that have been a family in Christ—**SHEKINAH Mission, The Good Shepherd City (TOGLM Int'l), and the family of Christ Healing Temple of God Deliverance Ministry**—you are part of my journey. Your consistent prayers have been heaven's reinforcement for my calling.

To my beloved late mother, **Paulina Egbadon**—your prayers have been fulfilled today. You stood by me day and night during my time of sickness, pouring love and hope into me when my body was weak. Your words, *"One hundred years is not forever,"* still echo as a reminder that love, faith, and sacrifice outlive time itself. Today, I stand as a living testimony of God's divine healing and miracle. Your faith lives on in every page of this book.

To **Dr. Leemon Ikpea**, a true father and pillar of support— thank you for your fatherly love, care, and constant encouragement. You have been there for me in profound and practical ways. I pray that God will reward your kindness and bless you abundantly in return.

Finally, to every reader who will pick up this book—you are an answer to prayer. May the words within draw you closer to God's purpose for your life and inspire you to build a family that Heaven can trust.

All glory to Jesus Christ forever. Amen.

📖 Introduction

Marriage is beautiful—but beauty alone cannot keep it standing.

If love alone were enough, no marriage would end in tears. If butterflies in your stomach could sustain a home, there would be no divorce, no broken vows, no children growing up in houses filled with silence instead of laughter.

This book was born out of a burden God placed in my heart—to prepare hearts not just for a wedding day, but for a lifetime of purposeful marriage. The counsel you'll read here is not theory. It is forged from my own life experiences, my victories and mistakes, my healing, and the stories of many I have counseled over the years. It is a blend of past, present, and God's divine plan for relationships that glorify Him.

I have seen marriages blossom into ministries, healing communities, and raising godly generations. I have also seen marriages collapse under the weight of unprepared hearts, selfish motives, and broken foundations. My prayer is that as you turn these pages, your eyes will be opened to truths that will save you years of pain and position you for lasting joy.

Whether you are single, preparing for marriage, or already married—this book is for you.

- If you are unmarried, it will help you choose with wisdom, not just emotion.
- If you are about to marry, it will help you lay a strong spiritual foundation that can withstand storms.

- If you are already married, it will call you back to God's original design—no matter how far things may have drifted.

Each chapter will challenge you, inspire you, and guide you through God's Word and real-life lessons. You will find reflection questions, prayers, and powerful truths that will echo in your heart long after you've closed the book.

This is not just a manual. It is a prophetic message. It is God's counsel for purposeful marriage.

So I invite you—read with an open heart. Allow the Holy Spirit to speak to you personally. And above all, be willing to obey the truths you encounter.

Because marriage is not just about finding the right person. It is about becoming the right person, so that together, you can fulfill God's assignment for your home.

Punch ✵

This is not a book you read and return to your shelf—it is a prophetic mirror.

As you look into it, God will show you who you truly are, who you should become, and who you must never join yourself to.

If you heed these words, your marriage will not just survive—it will become a sermon that preaches Christ to the world without you saying a word.

📔 CHAPTER 1

WHO ARE YOU BEFORE YOU SAY 'I DO'?

Discovering Your Identity in Christ Before Choosing a Life Partner

---

🕊️ □ *"You can't give what you don't have. Until you know who you are in Jesus Christ, you will not know what you need."*

◆ The Question of Identity

Long before vows are exchanged and rings are worn, there must be a solid answer to one question:

Who are you?

In a world where identity is often shaped by culture, family expectations, or social media trends, it's dangerously easy to walk into marriage as a stranger to yourself. Many broken homes didn't just start with the wrong partner—they began with an undefined purpose.

🎯 Identity Is the First Foundation

The first marriage in the Bible began with identity. God formed man and gave him purpose before He gave him a partner:

📖 *"And God said, Let us make man in our image, after our likeness...."* — Genesis 1:26

📖 *"Then the Lord God took the man and put him in the Garden of Eden to tend and keep it."* — Genesis 2:15

Adam wasn't just waiting around for Eve. He was working in his assignment. He was walking in intimacy with God. He understood who he was and why he existed—then God said, *"It is not good that the man should be alone..."*

Purpose precedes partnership.

You don't get married to find yourself. You get married because you already know who you are—and you're ready to join with someone who knows who they are too, for the sake of God's purpose.

🚫 The Danger of Entering Marriage Without Identity

Let's be honest—the world doesn't make this easy.

You're expected to marry:

- Because of age pressure
- Because "everyone is getting married"

- Because of family expectations
- Or simply because you're tired of being alone

But marriage without identity is like a journey without a map. You'll move, but you'll be lost.

Real-life story:

A woman married a man just because he was a church worker. But after five years, he lost interest in spiritual things, had affairs, and said his wife now "stinks." The foundation was weak because it was built on activity in church, not relationship with God.

📖 *"Having a form of godliness, but denying its power..." — 2 Timothy 3:5*

Don't confuse spiritual activity with spiritual maturity.

💡 You Are Not Just Male or Female — You Are a Light

As someone created in God's image, your identity is more than your gender, tribe, or title. You are the expression of Christ on earth. Jesus is the blueprint:

- His character — integrity, humility, boldness, sacrifice
- His purpose — to redeem, to lead, to serve
- His devotion — always connected to the Father

You are called to be light in a dark world. Your marriage is supposed to multiply that light—not dim it.

This is why God sends people out in partnership—two by two (Luke 10:1)—because companionship strengthens the mission.

📖 *"One shall chase a thousand, and two shall put ten thousand to flight..."* — *Deuteronomy 32:30*

So what happens when two people with no light come together?

It's not love—it's darkness multiplied.

🔥 Christ Is the Purpose. Peace Is the Reward.

The purpose of your life—and by extension, your marriage—must be centered on Christ. If it's centered on loneliness, money, sex, pressure, or just desire, it will collapse under weight it was never designed to carry.

📖 **"And His name shall be called... Prince of Peace."** — **Isaiah 9:6**

If Christ is not the purpose, then peace will not be the reward. Only the One who owns peace can sustain it in your home.

This is why assumption is dangerous. You cannot assume your partner will "change after marriage." You cannot assume "things will work themselves out." If the identity and values are not aligned before marriage, don't expect alignment afterward.

Real-life story:

A woman ignored the red flags of emotional coldness during courtship. After marriage, the man said he never planned for a sick wife—only children. Her health crisis became her loneliness, and almost her death. If Christ was the center, compassion and purpose would have spoken louder.

Reflection Questions

1. Do I know my identity in Christ apart from any relationship?
2. Am I walking in my God-given purpose before seeking a partner?
3. Am I looking for a marriage that multiplies light—or just fills a gap?
4. Is Christ truly the center of my life, or am I still seeking peace elsewhere?

🙏 Prayer

Lord, reveal to me who I am in You. Help me not to build my life or future on pressure, assumption, or emotion. Establish me in Your truth, in Your purpose, and prepare me for the kind of union that glorifies You. In Jesus' name, Amen.

CHAPTER 2

WHY DO YOU NEED A PART-NER?

Understanding God's Design for Companionship and Purpose Alignment

---

🕊️ □ *"Marriage is not a rescue plan for lonely people. It's a reinforcement plan for purpose-driven people."*

◈ The Myth of Completion

We've grown up with ideas like:

"I just need someone to complete me."

"Once I marry, my life will make sense."

Culture has wired many to believe that marriage is:

- The ultimate cure for loneliness
- The finish line of adulthood
- The final solution to a broken past

But here's a bold truth:

✴ *If you marry because you're empty, you will enter marriage as a burden.*

Marriage does not complete you — **God does.**

Marriage does not define you — **purpose does.**

Before you ask *"Who should I marry?"* you must ask:
"Why do I even need a partner in the first place?"

🎯 God's Original Blueprint: Partnership for Purpose

Let's return to the Garden.

📖 *"It is not good for the man to be alone. I will make him a helper suitable for him." — Genesis 2:18*

Notice — God didn't say Adam was lonely. Adam was working, naming animals, and communing with God. He was not idle or bored. Yet God said, *"not good."*

Why?

Because **purpose needs partnership.**

God never created marriage to solve emotional hunger. He created it to **multiply mission.** Adam had an assignment — and Eve was created to be a *helper suitable.*

The Hebrew word for helper is **ezer kenegdo** — a term used for military reinforcements and even for God Himself as a deliverer.

Your partner isn't just someone who loves you — they're someone who helps you fulfill God's call on your life

⃠ Marriage Is Not a Healing System

Many people walk into marriage expecting it to fix:

- Emotional wounds
- Childhood trauma
- Insecurity
- Financial struggle
- Spiritual weakness

But **marriage is not a rehabilitation center.**

✄ *"Marriage doesn't heal you — it reveals you."*

It brings to light what was hidden,
not to condemn you,
but to confront what you never allowed God to heal.

- If you're angry before marriage, anger will now have an audience.
- If you're insecure before marriage, marriage will expose it through comparison and fear.
- If you're undisciplined before marriage, the pressures of responsibility will magnify it.

Marriage doesn't cure emotional pain — it **mirrors** it.

That's why you must let Christ heal you *before* you say, "I do."

Emotional vulnerability in marriage is beautiful when it flows from **healing**, not from **brokenness**.
Otherwise, your wounds will keep asking your partner
to play the role only the Holy Spirit was designed to fill.

⚒ Purpose Alignment: Two for Ten Thousand

📖 *"Two are better than one, because they have a good reward for their labor." — Ecclesiastes 4:9*

📖 *"One will chase a thousand, and two will put ten thousand to flight." — Deuteronomy 32:30*

God's math is divine. When two people align in Christ, the result is not addition — it's **multiplication.**

Marriage multiplies:

- Vision
- Faith
- Power
- Generational impact

📖 *Real Story:*

A Christian woman once said, *"I married him because we clicked, but we never connected in calling."*
Now, she's passionate about missions and outreach; her husband wants a soft life and comfort. What she thought was love became a weight. They weren't aligned. They were just emotionally attached.
💡 *Attraction without alignment is deception.*

🚧 Not Everyone Is Your Helper

Here's the hard truth:

Not everyone who loves you is sent to help you.

Some people were sent to walk beside you for a season, but not to covenant with you for a lifetime. Helpers are not defined by how much you laugh with them — but by how much they strengthen your calling.

Compatibility	Purpose Alignment
We like the same things	We live for the same King
Easy to talk	Easy to pray
Shares hobbies	Shares vision
Follows emotions	Follows God's direction

Marriage is not choosing a fan — it's choosing a fellow soldier.

📖 *""She is your partner, the wife of your marriage covenant."." — Malachi 2:14*

🤝 Jesus Sent Them Two by Two

📖 *"After this the Lord appointed seventy-two others and sent them two by two ahead of him..." — Luke 10:1*

Why? Because:

- Ministry is more effective in unity
- Isolation invites vulnerability

- Two bring encouragement, accountability, and reinforcement

Marriage is your closest form of discipleship and mission. Your spouse must not be a distraction — they must be a **divine deployment.**

When your marriage is joined by heaven, it becomes a platform for evangelism, peace, and generational impact.

Reflection Questions

1. Am I looking for marriage to heal me or to partner with me in God's purpose?
2. Is the person I'm considering aligned with my assignment?
3. Do I know the difference between attraction and alignment?
4. Can I see God multiplying purpose through this relationship?

🙏 Prayer

Father, help me to desire what You designed. Deliver me from pressure, assumptions, and deception. Open my eyes to see the kind of helper that aligns with my calling. Heal every broken part of me that seeks marriage for rescue, and teach me to wait for covenant with wisdom and peace. In Jesus' name, Amen.

📖 CHAPTER 3

THE MARRIAGE BLUEPRINT: WHAT GOD REALLY HAD IN MIND

Uncovering the Divine Pattern That Modern Culture Forgot

🏠 *"You don't build a house by feeling inspired — you build it by following the architect's plan."*

Before there was culture, tradition, or wedding ceremonies… there was God — the Architect of marriage.
Before romance novels and wedding hashtags, there was a garden…
A man on assignment…
And a woman fashioned for purpose.

Today, marriages crash not only because love is missing, but because the **blueprint** is missing.
You can't expect God to bless a marriage He didn't design.

📖 Back to the Beginning: The Garden Template

Let's take a journey to Genesis 2 — the first marriage, the first love story, the original plan.

Here's what we often miss:

◈ **Adam had a relationship with God before Eve.**

"And the LORD God took the man, and put him into the garden of Eden to dress it and to keep it." — Genesis 2:15

He was planted in purpose. He was walking with God.
He wasn't "looking" for a wife — he was living in obedience.

⬤ **God didn't give Adam a woman because he was thirsty — He gave Adam a woman because he was ready.**

◈ **Adam had an assignment before he had a partner.**

He was naming animals, managing the Garden, and fulfilling divine responsibilities.
God watched Adam and said, *"It is not good for the man to be alone."*

Adam wasn't "lonely." He was complete in God.
But **purpose requires partnership.**
So, God designed a helper — not a fan, not a follower, but a divinely matched reinforcement.

Hebrew: *Ezer Kenegdo* — a strong helper, a partner in battle. The same word used when the Bible says *"God is our help."*

📖 The 4 Layers of God's Marriage Blueprint

1️⃣ Spiritual Foundation (God First)

Marriage is first spiritual, then emotional, then physical.
God must be the origin and the center of the union.

"Unless the LORD builds the house, they labor in vain who build it." — Psalm 127:1

Marriage without God is like building a mansion on sand.

2️⃣ Purpose Alignment (Why Are You Together?)

Eve was created to help Adam fulfill his calling — not to cure boredom.
Marriage must answer a **why**, not just a **who**.

⚠️ Marrying someone who doesn't share your vision is like tying two horses to opposite carts.

3️⃣ Order & Roles (Not Control — Responsibility)

Adam was made first — not to dominate, but to lead in responsibility.
Eve was made from his rib — not from his head (to rule over him), nor his feet (to be trampled), but from his side — to walk beside.

Biblical order is not about power. It's about function.

"Husbands, love your wives, just as Christ loved the church and gave Himself up for her." — Ephesians 5:25

4⬚ Naked and Not Ashamed (Transparency & Trust)

"And they were both naked, the man and his wife, and were not ashamed."— *Genesis 2:25*

This speaks of more than physical nudity. It means:

- Open communication
- Emotional vulnerability
- Spiritual accountability

If you can't be real with the one you want to marry, you're not ready to marry.

🔒 How Culture Has Broken the Blueprint

Modern relationships flip God's order:

1. They start with physical intimacy before spiritual compatibility
2. They prioritize romance over responsibility
3. They choose partners based on pressure and preference, not purpose

♀ Real Talk:

"He goes to church" ≠ "He's walking in divine purpose"
"She's beautiful" ≠ "She's built to help you fulfill your assignment"

If you don't follow God's process, you won't enjoy God's promise.

♨ What God Really Had in Mind

God's idea of marriage is not just two people falling in love — but two people falling in line with His will.

It's how love looks when shaped by heaven's assignment — not just human emotion.
It's two hearts aligned, building God's dream together.

A marriage where:

- Christ is King
- Love is sacrificial
- Purpose is central
- Generations are blessed

This is not a fairy tale.
This is **God's intention.**

💬 Real Story: The Couple That Waited for the Blueprint

A young woman once shared:

"We were in love, but we didn't rush. We fasted and prayed for months, sought counsel, and served in church together. God revealed we were meant to do ministry as a couple. Now, we're mentoring others and raising kingdom children."

Love wasn't enough.
Clarity, conviction, and calling made the difference.

💬 Real Story: When Beauty Isn't the Blueprint

There was a man who met a woman that seemed perfect—at least on the surface. She was beautiful, light-skinned, stylish, and spoke with confidence. He was drawn in by her appearance and charm. They connected quickly, even did medical tests—blood group and genotype matched. Physically and emotionally, she seemed ideal. They became intimate, and he was convinced she was "the one."

But beneath the surface, cracks began to show.

Her family dynamics were troubling. She had a deep craving for money, her mother's influence was overwhelming, and her spending habits were extravagant. One of the first things she did was criticize his wardrobe—she replaced his clothes without asking and condemned his style. His siblings noticed and asked, "Can you really cope with her?"

But he was blinded—by beauty, by chemistry, by the illusion of compatibility.

They moved forward with family introductions and began preparing for marriage. But he was financially drained, trying to keep up with her lifestyle. Unknown to him, his father was praying: *"Lord, if this is Your will, let the marriage hold. But if not, let it be stopped."*

Then came the moment of truth.

She told him she was no longer interested—because she didn't like his style of worship. He was stunned. Around that time, her mother had begun demanding items for the wedding that far exceeded his budget. It became clear: this wasn't a partnership—it was a performance.

Eventually, the plans collapsed. She walked away.
And then, after that storm passed, his wife came.

🌐 What You Must Understand

- **Attraction is not assignment.** Just because someone looks good doesn't mean they're good for your purpose.
- **Compatibility is more than chemistry.** You need spiritual alignment, not just emotional excitement.
- **God's blueprint protects you.** My father's prayer was a shield I didn't even know I needed.

💭 Reflection Questions

1. Am I following God's order or culture's chaos?
2. Do I know the purpose of marriage according to Scripture?
3. Is the person I'm considering someone who aligns with God's plan — or just my preference?

🙏 Prayer

Father, restore Your blueprint in my heart. Help me unlearn the lies of culture and receive Your truth. Build my future home on the foundation of Your Word. Help me wait for the one You designed to walk with me in purpose. In Jesus' name, Amen.

📖 CHAPTER 4

THEN VS. NOW: WHAT THE BI-BLE SAYS ABOUT MARRIAGE THAT YOU'VE NEVER HEARD IN CHURCH

Uncovering the Timeless Truths and the Modern Myths We've Accepted Without Question

---

💬 *"The problem is not that we don't know the Bible... it's that we've replaced it with culture and called it Christianity."*

We love quoting wedding verses like:

"What God has joined together, let no man separate."

But... do we know what God actually joins together?

If we're honest, most of our relationship beliefs are a strange cocktail of:

- Bible verses taken out of context
- Romantic movie scripts

- Cultural pressure
- Social media trends

And then we wonder why marriages collapse under the weight of unmet expectations.

📖 The Then: God's Original Picture

From Genesis to Revelation, marriage was never just about love — it was about **covenant**.

In the Old Testament:

- Marriage was a spiritual contract before it was a social celebration
- It was rooted in family legacy and divine purpose, not just personal happiness
- God often compared His relationship with Israel to a husband with a bride

> *"Your Maker is your husband…"* — *Isaiah 54:5*

> *"I will betroth you to Me forever…"* — *Hosea 2:19*

In the New Testament:

- Marriage became a living sermon about Christ and the Church
- Husbands were called to love sacrificially — not just romantically
- Wives were called to respect deeply — not just emotionally

Marriage was never casual. It was **holy ground**.

⚠ The Now: Where We've Gone Off-Script

Modern culture has:

1. Replaced covenant with convenience
2. Traded God's blueprint for personal preference
3. Made weddings more important than the marriage itself

🔑 Real Talk:

Many couples prepare for the **day** instead of preparing for the **life**.

They study color palettes, menus, and hashtags… but neglect prayer, purpose, and discipleship.

🔑 What We've Missed in Church Teaching

Here are truths we rarely hear from the pulpit:

1. **Marriage is a calling — not an escape plan.**
   If God hasn't called you to it, you'll treat it like a prison instead of a platform.
2. **Love alone is not the foundation — Christ is.**
   Without Him at the center, your best efforts will still crack under pressure.
3. **Your spouse is not your source — God is.**
   Expecting them to meet every need will drain the relationship dry.

4. **Biblical roles are about function, not competition.**
   God's order is not outdated — it's the operating system for a healthy marriage.

🛠 Bridging the Then and the Now

If we want marriages that last, we must return to the Architect's plan:

- Seek God first — before seeking a partner
- Align with purpose — not just preference
- Build on covenant — not just chemistry
- Live marriage as ministry — not just companionship

💡 Example: The Couple That Chose Mission Over Mood

A couple I know decided that before they ever discussed wedding details, they'd first write a **ministry vision** for their marriage.

They asked:
"What will our union do for the Kingdom?"
Ten years later, their love is still strong — because their foundation was **mission**, not **mood**.

💬 Reflection Questions

1. Have I replaced God's truth with cultural opinions about marriage?
2. Do I know the biblical "why" for marriage — or just the emotional "want"?

3. What changes must I make now to align my relationship with God's blueprint?

🙏 Prayer

Lord, open my eyes to see marriage as You see it.
Help me unlearn the lies I've embraced and return to Your truth.
Give me the courage to build my future on covenant, not convenience.
Let my marriage — present or future — reflect Christ to the world. Amen.

CHAPTER 5

YOUR MARRIAGE IS A MINISTRY — EVEN IF YOU'RE NOT A PASTOR

Why Your Home Must Become an Altar of Evangelism, Love, and Power

---

💬 *"The first church your children will ever attend is your home."*

Some people think ministry is reserved for preachers with microphones, worship leaders on stage, or missionaries traveling across continents.

But the truth is — if you're married, you already have a ministry.

It's called **your home**.

📖 The First Church Wasn't a Building

After the resurrection of Christ, when persecution scattered the apostles, the early believers didn't stop gathering — they simply moved the gathering into their homes.

"They broke bread from house to house…" — *Acts 2:46*

Before pulpits, there were communion tables.
Before sermons, there were house fellowships.
Before choirs, there were families singing psalms together.

The Apostle Paul reinforced this principle:

"If anyone does not know how to manage his own household, how will he take care of the church of God?" — *1 Timothy 3:5*

In God's order, **family leadership comes before public leadership**.
The home is the proving ground for the pulpit.

♀ Eden Was the First Sanctuary

The Garden of Eden wasn't just a beautiful garden — it was the first meeting place between God and humanity.
Adam and Eve's marriage was designed to be a living example of God's covenant love.

Your marriage is not just about romance.
It's a **gospel on display**.
When the world looks at your union, they should see:

- Christ's love for the church (*Ephesians 5:25*)
- Unity in diversity
- Sacrifice without selfishness
- Forgiveness without conditions

⚜ Marriage Preaches Without Words

Whether you know it or not, your marriage is telling a story. The question is: **Which one?**

- When you love sacrificially in hard seasons — you preach Christ's perseverance
- When you extend grace after failure — you preach the cross
- When you honor each other in public and private — you preach God's faithfulness

✎ *"Your marriage is either a platform for the gospel or a billboard for dysfunction."*

⬡ The Danger of a Silent Pulpit

Some couples think, *"As long as we're together, we're fine."*
But a silent marriage — one that hides love, avoids prayer, and neglects discipleship — is like a church building with no worship inside.
God designed marriage to be a **living altar**:

- Where prayer is normal, not awkward
- Where scripture is read, not just scrolled past
- Where hospitality is offered, not just selfies taken

♀ Real Story: A Home That Became God's Meeting Place

A couple in my neighborhood opens their home every Saturday for fellowship and Bible study.

They aren't pastors, but they've created a space where neighbors feel the presence of God.

People come, share meals, worship, and hear the Word — and many lives have been transformed simply because their home became **God's meeting place**.

📝 My Own Marriage Lesson

Sometimes, misunderstandings happen in my house — something we all know is unavoidable.

But the ability for my wife and I to manage it brings out the beauty of purpose.

We have morning and evening devotions daily, so there's no way I can continue quarreling.

I must say, *"I'm sorry,"* because we cannot study and fellowship in disunity.

"Husbands, live with your wives in an understanding way... so that your prayers will not be hindered." — 1 Peter 3:7

If my relationship with my wife is strained, my relationship with God will be hindered.

Unity at home is not optional — it's a spiritual necessity.

🏠 Practical Ways to Turn Your Home Into a Ministry

1. Pray together daily — even if it's just 5 minutes before bed

2. Host people with love — a warm meal can open a
    heart to the gospel
3. Teach by living — let your children see how you re-
    solve conflict biblically
4. Support missions — give, pray, and partner with
    those spreading the gospel

⚔️ Spiritual Warfare in the Living Room

The enemy hates marriages that glorify God because they re-
produce both physically (*children*) and spiritually (*disciples*).
That's why healthy Christian homes face intense attacks —
arguments, coldness, distractions.

This is not just "marriage problems" — this is **ministry warfare**.
Guard your home like a shepherd guards his flock.

💭 Reflection Questions

1. If my marriage was the only sermon my children ever
    heard, what gospel would they believe?
2. Are we actively using our home to serve God's mis-
    sion?
3. What needs to change for our home to reflect God's
    heart?

🙏 Prayer

**Father, thank You for trusting me with the ministry of
marriage.**
Help me to see my home as Your altar.

Fill our conversations, decisions, and habits with Your presence.
Teach us to love in a way that preaches the gospel without words.
Let our union become a light that draws others to You.
In Jesus' name, Amen.

CHAPTER 6

WHAT NO ONE TOLD YOU ABOUT CHILDREN, BROKEN HOMES, AND GENERATIONAL PAIN

How Your Marriage Shapes Your Children Before They're Even Born

---

💬 *"You're not just raising children — you're raising generations."*

We often think parenting begins after the wedding, after the pregnancy, or after the first baby is born.
But in God's eyes, the foundation for raising godly children is laid **before they even arrive** — in the way a husband and wife live, love, and align in purpose.

If marriage is the first church, then children are the first disciples.

🎯 The Silent Classroom Called Home

Your children will learn more about God's love, mercy, forgiveness, and justice from how you treat each other than from the sermons you take them to hear on Sunday.

- They will learn how a man should treat a woman by watching their father
- They will learn how a woman should honor and respect a man by watching their mother
- They will learn forgiveness by seeing you forgive each other
- They will learn prayer by hearing you pray together

Even your silence teaches.

📖 God's Plan for Generational Blessing

"These words that I command you today shall be on your heart. You shall teach them diligently to your children..." — Deuteronomy 6:6–7

Parenting in the kingdom is not a random event — it's a **daily transfer of truth**.

God designed families to pass down faith like an inheritance, so each generation knows Him better than the last.
But the enemy also knows this... and he works just as hard to pass down brokenness.

⚠ The Cycle of Generational Pain

When a home is full of anger, abuse, infidelity, or neglect, those patterns don't just stop with the parents — they often repeat in the children's lives.

- A father who abandons his children may have come from a home where his father abandoned him
- A mother who struggles to trust her husband may have grown up watching betrayal
- Children who see constant fighting may grow up believing that's "just how marriage is"

If these cycles are not broken in Christ, they become **invisible chains**, binding generation after generation.

♀ The Power of Purpose Before Parenting

The story of Manoah and his wife in Judges 13 is a perfect example.

When the angel appeared to announce the birth of Samson, they didn't just rejoice — they asked:

"What is to be the child's manner of life, and what is his mission?"

If they were not already walking in purpose, they wouldn't have had the wisdom to ask such a question.

And if God had found them out of alignment, perhaps the message wouldn't have come to them at all.

The same is true with Joseph and Mary.

God chose that family to be highly favored because He already knew Joseph would stand in purpose beside Mary — even when he thought she had betrayed him.

Purpose kept him from abandoning her.

Purpose protected the destiny of the Savior.

Your alignment with God **before children arrive** determines the spiritual inheritance they will receive **when they do**.

🖳 Real Story: The Home That Preached Without Words

A teenage boy once told me:

"I've never seen my parents shout at each other. They don't hide disagreements from us, but they solve them quickly. It's like they guard our peace on purpose."

That boy wasn't quoting Bible verses — he was quoting what he saw at home.
His parents' marriage became a **living sermon**, and he was listening.

✂ Breaking the Cycle

If you came from a broken home, hear this:
You can start a new chapter for your family line.
Here's how:

- **Healing in Christ** — Forgive your parents if they failed you. Carrying their offense will make you repeat their patterns
- **Renewing Your Mind** — Replace cultural lies about marriage and parenting with God's truth
- **Living by Example** — Be the spouse and parent you wish you had growing up

💬 Reflection Questions

1. What patterns from my family background do I see in my current relationship?

2. Am I actively creating a home where my future children will learn Christ naturally?
3. Have I prayed over my children's destiny — even before they're born?

🙏 Prayer

Father, thank You for trusting me with the gift of family. Heal every brokenness from my past that could harm the next generation.

Teach me to love my spouse in a way that teaches our children the gospel without words.

Let our home be a place of peace, purpose, and generational blessing.

In Jesus' name, Amen.

📓 CHAPTER 7

THE TRIANGLE THAT KEEPS MARRIAGES FROM BREAKING

Man + Woman + God = The Unbreakable Formula for Lasting Love

💬 *"A marriage without God is like a tripod missing its third leg — it will wobble until it collapses."*

📖 The Heavenly Equation

Marriage isn't just about two people agreeing to live together. In God's design, it's a **covenant triangle**:
- Husband
- Wife
- **God at the top point**

When either spouse tries to remove God from the top point, the triangle collapses into a fragile line that can easily break.

From the beginning, God designed marriage to be a **three-way covenant,** not a two-way contract.

Without the third Person in the equation, love becomes de-
pendent on moods, willpower, and fleeting emotions — all
of which change.

But when God is at the top point, love is anchored in something **unshakable**.

▲ Why the Triangle Works

Think of marriage as an **equilateral triangle**:

- God is at the top point
- Husband and wife are at the two bottom points

The closer each spouse moves toward God, the closer they
move toward each other.
Your personal walk with God directly impacts the health of
your marriage.

📖 *"A cord of three strands is not quickly broken."* —
Ecclesiastes 4:12

That "third strand" is not just a feeling — it's **God Himself**.

⚔ Three Pillars That Keep the Triangle Strong

1 Mutual Submission to God's Word

Before you submit to each other, you must both submit to
God.

"Submit to one another out of reverence for Christ." —
Ephesians 5:21

2⃞ Prayer as a Couple

Prayer isn't just for crises — it's **daily maintenance** for the
marriage.
Couples who pray together disarm bitterness before it takes
root.

3⃞ Purpose Partnership

Marriage is more than sharing a bed or bills — it's about
sharing a mission.
When both are aligned in purpose, storms won't easily tear
them apart.

💬 Real Story: A Family Friend on the Verge of Breaking Apart

I once had a family friend — a good man, a social worker,
married for just a year, blessed with a child.
His work kept him busy with one event after another, leaving
little time for his family.

One Sunday morning, while preparing my sermon, I felt God
prompting me to call him.
When he answered, I could hear noise and tension in the
background. I asked if everything was fine.
He tried to cover it up, but I could tell something wasn't
right.

I asked, *"Do you have daily devotion — morning and evening — in
your home?"*

He said, *"We do pray."*

I explained, *"Prayer is asking God for something. Devotion and fellowship are doing God's bidding.*
It's like a child asking his father for a biscuit, and the father saying, 'Have you done the task I gave you before asking for a treat?'"

He paused… then admitted they'd been missing that element.

I counseled him on living a **purpose-driven marriage** — reminding him that even as a social worker, there are ways to impact the next generation while still raising a strong family.

That conversation shifted his perspective.
He began leading consistent devotions in his home, and it saved their marriage from heading toward a quiet collapse.

⬣ The Devotion Gap

Many Christian homes are struggling not because they lack prayer, but because they lack **fellowship**.

- Prayer talks to God
- Fellowship walks with Him
- Prayer is communication
- Fellowship is alignment

When devotion is absent, God's presence fades from the top point of the marriage triangle — and that's when cracks begin to show.

○ Reflection Questions

- Is God truly at the top point of my marriage, or just a guest on special occasions?
- Am I growing closer to God personally — so I can grow closer to my spouse?
- Do we have both prayer and fellowship in our home?

🙏 Prayer

Lord, I don't want my marriage to be a two-legged table.
Be the third cord that binds us together.
Teach us to value fellowship as much as prayer.
Draw us closer to You so we can draw closer to each other.
In Jesus' name, Amen.

📖 CHAPTER 8

WHAT HAPPENS WHEN GOD CAN'T SEE HIMSELF IN YOUR HOME ANYMORE

*When love, sacrifice, and purpose go missing —
and how to find them again*

💬 *"A marriage without God's reflection becomes a house with lights on but no warmth inside."*

🕊 The Mirror Effect

Marriage was designed to be a **living reflection** of God's relationship with His people — full of:

- Love
- Faithfulness
- Sacrifice
- Purpose

God wants to love the man **through his wife**, and the woman **through her husband**.

They become His lens — seeing each other with the eyes of God.

This reciprocal respect **welcomes God's presence** into fellowship.

When He looks into your home, He's meant to see Himself:

- 🫀 His love in the way you speak to each other
- 🕊 His patience in the way you handle conflict
- 🤲 His generosity in the way you give without keeping score

But what happens when He looks… and doesn't recognize Himself there anymore?

🔄 Signs God's Reflection Is Missing

1️⃣ Love becomes conditional
Affection is given only when the other person "deserves" it.

2️⃣ Sacrifice disappears
Spouses focus more on what they're getting than what they're giving.

3️⃣ Purpose is forgotten
The marriage turns inward, losing sight of its mission to impact others and glorify God.-

🔍 Bible Insight

📖 *"You have forsaken the love you had at first. Consider how far you have fallen! Repent and do the things you did at first."* — *Revelation 2:4–5*

This was God's message to the church in Ephesus — and it applies to marriage.

If God's presence feels far, it's not because He moved — it's because **we stopped reflecting Him**.

💬 Real Story: When the Lens Went Cloudy

I visited a home where the couple still went to church faithfully, had a well-presented family in public, and prayed together in the congregation — but in private, their relationship felt... cold.

God had become an **event** in their marriage, not a **daily presence**.

I spoke with the wife and said:

"God doesn't just want to be invited for special occasions — He wants to live in your home."

Her husband was a Minister of God — but **titles don't guarantee spiritual depth**.

We prayed together, and soon she began having spiritual revelations in dreams — visions of attacks on their ministry and family.

Then came a severe financial crisis. It wasn't just bad luck — it was **spiritual warfare**.

When God's reflection fades from the marriage, the enemy moves quickly to **distort the image**.

If he can break the mirror (the marriage), he can block the light (God's glory) from shining into the next generation.

🛠 How to Restore God's Reflection in Your Home

1☐ Repent and return to first works
Go back to the habits you had when your love for God and each other was fresh.

2☐ Rebuild spiritual intimacy
Pray together, worship together, and study the Word together.

3☐ Live outwardly focused
Serve together — in your community, in your church, in your street.
Marriage thrives when it's part of a mission **bigger than itself.**

4☐ Guard your home spiritually
Be alert to subtle shifts — coldness, resentment, pride — and deal with them before they become strongholds.

💭 Reflection Questions

- If God visited my home today, would He see Himself in our love, patience, and purpose?
- Have I allowed routine, pride, or busyness to dim God's reflection in my marriage?
- Are there any spiritual cracks the enemy could be using to weaken our foundation?

🙏 Prayer

Lord, search my home and my heart.

If You cannot see Yourself here, show me what needs to change.

Restore love where it has grown cold, sacrifice where it has become selfish, and purpose where it has been forgotten.

Protect our home from every plan of the enemy.

Let our marriage be a true reflection of You.

In Jesus' name, Amen.

CHAPTER 9

BROKEN BUT BLESSED: BIBLE COUPLES WHO GOT IT RIGHT

"God doesn't use perfect couples — He perfects surrendered couples."

□ *"Heaven doesn't need perfection to build legacy—just obedience."*

📖 The Beauty in Imperfect Stories

When you read the Bible, you quickly realize that God's "model couples" were far from flawless.

- They had fears
- They made bad decisions
- They faced family drama

Yet the common thread wasn't perfection — it was **alignment with God's purpose**.

Their obedience, even when imperfect, positioned them for blessings that **outlived them**

🔍 Case Study 1: Manoah and His Wife (Judges 13)

Manoah and his wife couldn't have children — until an angel showed up with a promise:
They would have a son who would begin to deliver Israel from the Philistines.

What stands out?

- They didn't just celebrate the good news — they asked how to raise the child in God's way *before* he was born.
- Their **spiritual alignment** made them trustworthy stewards of the miracle.
- **Purpose prepared them** for the promise.

🔍 Case Study 2: Joseph and Mary *(Matthew 1:18–25)*

Joseph discovered Mary was pregnant — and he knew he wasn't the father.
By Jewish law, he could have exposed her publicly.

But Joseph was a man of **quiet righteousness**.

- God already knew his character — which is why He chose Joseph's home for Jesus.
- When the angel explained the truth, Joseph didn't hesitate.
- He protected, supported, and loved Mary through the scandal.

- He kept his family **aligned with God's mission**, even when the world misunderstood.

🔍 Case Study 3: Abraham and Sarah *(Genesis 12–21)*

They weren't perfect.

- Sarah laughed at God's promise.
- Abraham tried to "help God out" by having a child with Hagar.

Yet they kept returning to God's instructions.

- They built altars.
- They obeyed again, even after failing.
- God **renamed them, renewed His promise**, and gave them Isaac — proof that His covenant can still stand after our mistakes.

💡 The Thread That Ties Them Together

In every case, these couples:

- Lived with **shared purpose**
- Responded to **God's voice**
- Stayed **aligned**, even in the face of fear, confusion, or public misunderstanding

💬 *God doesn't bless a home because it's scandal-free — He blesses it because it's purpose-driven.*

◯ Reflection Questions

1. Am I aligning my relationship with God's purpose before asking Him for blessings?
2. Could God trust my home with a mission that impacts generations?
3. Do I value alignment with my spouse as much as I value answers to prayer?

🙏 Prayer

Lord, I may not have a perfect marriage, but I want a surrendered one.

Help us to be like Manoah and his wife, Joseph and Mary, Abraham and Sarah — ready to hear You, quick to obey, and united in purpose.

Align us with Your mission so our home can be trusted with Your blessing.

In Jesus' name, Amen.

📓 CHAPTER 10

MARRIAGE UNDER PRESSURE: WHAT COUNSELORS WISH YOU KNEW BEFORE SAYING "I DO"

"A wedding lasts a day; a marriage lasts a lifetime. Don't prepare for the party and forget the partnership."

📞☐ *"Pressure doesn't break a marriage — it reveals what it was built on."*

📖 Pressure Points in Modern Marriages

Every marriage will face pressure — but **pressure alone doesn't destroy a relationship**.
It's the **unprepared heart** that buckles under it.

Before saying "I do," you need more than love.

You need:

- 🧠 Wisdom
- 👀 Awareness

- 💪 Courage to confront uncomfortable truths

Even Spirit-filled couples are not immune to red flags:

- Wrong motives for marriage
- Unrealistic expectations
- Silent killers like pride, unforgiveness, or unspoken resentment

📖 *"Suppose one of you wants to build a tower. Won't you first sit down and estimate the cost to see if you have enough money to complete it?" — Luke 14:28*

Marriage is no different — **count the cost before you start building**.

🪦 Five Silent Killers of Peace in Marriage

1️⃣ Marrying to Escape
Marriage multiplies whatever is already in your life — joy or pain.
Don't marry to escape loneliness, pressure, or hardship.

2️⃣ Ignoring Red Flags
Bad patterns don't disappear after the wedding.
If you excuse them now, they'll intensify later.

3️⃣ Unequally Yoked Purpose
When your life callings point in opposite directions, tension becomes constant.

4️⃣ Poor Conflict Management

Without healthy disagreement, small issues become spiritual wars.

5 ⬜ Neglecting the God Factor

Prayer without purpose is powerless.
Devotion without love is hollow.
God must be more than a wedding guest — He must be the **architect of your home**.

💬 Real Story: A Lesson in the Barber's Chair

I took my four-year-old son to the barbing salon.
After his haircut, I handed him my phone (with parental controls).
The barber was surprised when my son unlocked it and asked, *"Does he know your password?"*

I smiled: *"Yes, he does. That's the relationship we have."*

I teach my son by example — including in the ways of the Lord.
The barber was amazed. Then he said, *"I want to get married so I can also have a son like this."*

As we talked, I discovered he admired my life but felt ashamed — all his siblings were married, and he wasn't.

I told him plainly:

"Don't get married because of pressure or circumstances. Seek your purpose, then search out your God-given partner.

Many make the mistake of trying to live someone else's life.
Understand the principles behind the lifestyle you admire before you try to copy it."

That day, I saw how easily people are moved toward marriage for the wrong reasons — not love, not purpose, but **comparison and pressure**.

📖 The Apostle Paul's Warning About Rushed Marriages

In *1 Corinthians 7:32–35*, Paul advised believers to remain unmarried unless they're ready to serve God **without distraction**.

He wasn't anti-marriage — he was **pro-purpose**.

Paul understood:

- Marriage brings blessings
- Marriage brings responsibilities
- Wrong motives can hinder your walk with God

His point still stands: **purpose should guide your choice**, not pressure.

⚒ How to Prepare Your Heart Before Marriage

- 🙏 Pray for discernment more than for a wedding date
- 👥 Seek godly counsel and be open to correction

- 🎯 Test your unity in purpose before testing your guest list
- 🤝 Learn conflict resolution rooted in grace and truth

💭 Reflection Questions

1. Am I entering marriage to build a life, or just to escape my current life?
2. Are there any warning signs I've been ignoring because of fear or pressure?
3. Do we have a shared vision from God for our marriage?

🙏 Prayer

Lord, help me prepare for marriage with wisdom, patience, and truth.
Expose every wrong motive, heal every insecurity, and align my heart with Your purpose.
Build my future home on a foundation that pressure cannot shake.
In Jesus' name, Amen.

CHAPTER 11

DON'T SETTLE — THE TRAP OF AGE, FAMILY, AND CHURCH PRESSURE

Why marrying too fast, too blind, or too scared will hurt more than waiting

---

"Pressure can tempt you to settle — but purpose gives you the strength to wait."

The Pressure Cooker of Marriage Decisions

In many cultures, **age is treated like an alarm clock** — if you're not married by a certain time, people act like something is wrong with you.

- Family members whisper
- Friends drop "hints"
- Church leaders may suggest you're "delaying God's will"

But the pressure isn't just external — it's internal too.

- You start counting birthdays instead of blessings

- You compare your timeline to others
- You make life decisions to quiet people's voices, not because you've heard **God's voice**

💔 The Price of Rushed Decisions

When you rush into marriage to meet a deadline — cultural, family, or church — you risk building your home on **sand**.

It may look fine at first, but **storms will reveal the cracks**.

I've counseled many who ignored red flags because they felt they "had no time to waste."

- One confessed: *"I thought if I didn't marry him now, no one else would come."*
- Another admitted: *"The church conducted marriage counselling without my spouse before we got married; I didn't want to exit because we had gone too far in the wedding preparations."*

💬 *Marriage is not a race — it's a lifetime covenant.*

If you let pressure replace prayer, you will exchange peace for regret.

📖 Case Study — "Mummy's Boy"

She thought she was marrying a man — but she married **a man and his mother**.

From day one:

- His mother decided where the furniture would sit

68

- How money would be spent
- Even how the couple would use their bedroom

Every decision passed through his mother first.

When the wife complained, the husband became **physically abusive**.

Instead of protecting her, he protected the interference.

⚠ Reference to the Triangle of Marriage

Recall *The Triangle That Keeps Marriages From Breaking*:

- God at the top
- Husband and wife at the base

This home had **another human** at the top.
Without God's leadership and unity at the base, the marriage lacked a **stable foundation**.

💡 Punchlines to Remember

- Pressure-driven marriages are regret-driven marriages
- If God isn't leading your choice, you're walking into a storm unprepared
- The only third party in your marriage should be **God**

❓ Reflection Questions

1. Have I ever considered marriage because of pressure rather than purpose?

2. Am I willing to delay a wedding if God shows me red flags?
3. What voices have the most influence on my relationship decisions — God's or people's?
4. If I married today, who would be at the top of my triangle — God or someone else?

🙏 Prayer

Lord, deliver me from the fear of delay and the pressure of people.
Teach me to wait for Your perfect timing and to hear Your voice above every other.
Prepare me for the partner You have chosen and help me build my home with You as the foundation.
In Jesus' name, Amen.

📖 CHAPTER 12

FINAL WORDS: IF YOU MISS EVERYTHING ELSE, REMEMBER THIS

A prayer, a charge, and a blessing for your future home

🏚️☐ *"If you forget every page, remember this: God doesn't just want you to marry — He wants you to build something eternal."*

🔥 Opening Hook

Let me leave you with this truth:

Your wedding day will last a few hours, but your marriage will **echo into eternity**.

It's not the gown, the suit, the cake, or the guest list that Heaven records —

It's the **covenant you make** and how you honor it.

💬 *I've poured my heart into these pages not so you can simply say "I do," but so you can stand before God years from now and hear Him say, "Well done."*

📖 The Final Scripture Anchor

📖 *"Therefore everyone who hears these words of mine and puts them into practice is like a wise man who built his house on the rock."* — *Matthew 7:24 (NIV)*

Your marriage will stand or fall based on what it's built on:

- ✗ Not emotions
- ✗ Not cultural pressure
- ✗ Not family expectations
- ✅ But **God's Word**

💬 The Last Story of 'Man' and 'Woman'

When I think of the couple we called "Man" and "Woman," my heart aches — not just for them, but for every home where **God's blueprint was ignored**.

They began with:

- Love
- Shared faith
- Deep prayers

But they also had **blind spots** they refused to address.

72

Small cracks were left unattended, and when the storm came, the house could not stand.

💬 *It's not the storm that destroys a marriage — it's the foundation you laid before the storm came.*

⚒ Your Covenant Checklist

Before you walk into marriage, carry these last instructions with you:

- ▲ Keep God at the top point of your marriage — the One both of you move toward
- 🛡 Protect your oneness. No friend, parent, or pastor should divide what God joined
- ♡ Guard your heart daily. Your spouse should always have your first loyalty after God
- 🙏 Pray together, not just for each other. Agreement in prayer is a weapon against every enemy of your home
- 💍 Choose love daily. Love is not a feeling — it's a **covenant action**

💎 Final Punchlines

- Marriage is not about how you start — it's about **who you become together**
- The devil doesn't fear your wedding day; he fears your **prayer life as a couple**
- A **God-built home** can survive any storm

Reflection Questions

- If storms came to my marriage tomorrow, would my foundation hold?
- Am I truly ready to love as Christ loves the Church — sacrificially and unconditionally?
- What boundaries do I need to set now to protect my future covenant?

🙏 Final Prayer

Lord, I hand over my current or future marriage into Your hands.
Be the foundation, the builder, and the keeper of my home.
Give me wisdom to choose rightly, strength to stand faithfully,
and a heart to love like You love me.
May my home be a light in a dark world,
and may our union preach the Gospel without words in Jesus' name, Amen.

✨ Blessing

- I bless your heart with **courage to believe again**
- I bless your home with **unity, joy, and protection**
- I bless your waiting with **patience and peace**
- And I declare — your marriage will not just survive; it will **thrive in God's purpose**

❖ DECLARATIONS OVER MY LIFE AND FUTURE HOME ❖

Read these aloud daily until they become the atmosphere you live in.

◈ I Declare…

1. I am whole in Christ, and my identity is unshakable.
2. I will not marry out of fear, pressure, or desperation—my steps are ordered by the Lord.
3. My marriage will glorify God, reflect His Kingdom, and advance His purposes on earth.
4. I am prepared spiritually, emotionally, and mentally for the covenant God has for me.
5. No generational curse or past pain will dictate my future—I am free indeed.
6. God will give me a partner who loves Him first and loves me faithfully.
7. My home will be a place of prayer, joy, and divine protection.
8. My children (born or unborn) will walk in God's ways and fulfill their destiny.
9. I reject every lie of the enemy against my relationships—truth, peace, and love will reign.
10. I will finish well in love, life, and purpose, in Jesus' name.

🍃 Key Verse

"The blessing of the Lord, it maketh rich, and He addeth no sorrow with it."

— Proverbs 10:22

📖 Instruction

Print these declarations. Keep them in your prayer corner. Say them over yourself every morning and before important relationship decisions.

ABOUT THE AUTHOR

Prophet Ose-Akhumen Momoh is a prophetic voice called by God with a mandate to bring healing, restoration, and deliverance to this generation. His ministry is marked by the power of the Holy Spirit to mend the brokenhearted, set captives free, and turn the hearts of men and women back to God. With an unwavering emphasis on holiness and righteousness, he carries a burden to see people walk in purity, truth, and divine purpose.

For years, Prophet Ose-akhumen Momoh has served as a counselor, teacher, and mentor to singles, couples, and families, guiding them through the difficult realities of identity, marriage, and destiny. His prophetic insight and compassionate heart have made him a trusted vessel in God's hands — bringing hope where despair once lived, restoration where homes were broken, and revival where hearts had grown cold.

More than a preacher, Prophet Ose-akhumen Momoh is a father, teacher, and reformer. His message goes beyond church walls, calling believers to see their lives, marriages, and families as living altars of worship and evangelism. Through healing, deliverance, and the ministry of God's Word, he continues to raise a generation that will reflect Christ and advance His Kingdom in every sphere of life.

www.ingramcontent.com/pod-product-compliance
Lightning Source LLC
LaVergne TN
LVHW041234080426
835508LV00011B/1209